The Federalist Papers

Bethany Bryan

America's Most Important Documents

Inquiry into Historical Sources

Cavendish Square
New York

Published in 2019 by Cavendish Square Publishing, LLC
243 5th Avenue, Suite 136, New York, NY 10016

First Edition

Website: cavendishsq.com

Library of Congress Cataloging-in-Publication Data

Names: Bryan, Bethany, author.
Title: The Federalist papers / Bethany Bryan.
Description: First edition. | New York : Cavendish Square, 2018. |
Series: America's most important documents: inquiry into historical sources | Includes bibliographical references and index.
Identifiers: LCCN 2018000495 (print) | LCCN 2018000756 (ebook) | ISBN 9781502636089 (eBook) | ISBN 9781502636072 (library bound) | ISBN 9781502636096 (pbk.)
Subjects: LCSH: Federalist--Juvenile literature. | Constitutional history--United States--Juvenile literature. | United States--Politics and government--1783-1789--Juvenile literature. | Federal government--United States--History--18th century--Juvenile literature.
Classification: LCC KF4515 (ebook) | LCC KF4515 .B79 2018 (print) | DDC 342.7302/4--dc23
LC record available at https://lccn.loc.gov/2018000495

Editorial Director: David McNamara
Editor: Kristen Susienka
Copy Editor: Alex Tessman
Associate Art Director: Amy Greenan
Designer: Joe Parenteau
Production Coordinator: Karol Szymczuk
Photo Research: J8 Media

The photographs in this book are used by permission and through the courtesy of: Cover, p. 47 GraphicaArts/Archive Photos/Getty Images; pp. 4, 28 Stock Montage/Getty Images; p. 7 Naturbild/Johner/Superstock.com; pp. 9, 20 Bettmann/Getty Images; pp. 10, 12 Hulton Archive/Getty Images; pp. 14, 51 Everett Historical/Shutterstock.com; p. 16 ClassicStock.com/Superstock.com; p. 18 DeAgostini/Getty Images; p. 22 3LH/SuperStock; p. 25 National Portrait Gallery, Washington/http://www.npg.si.edu/exh/brush/ben.htm/File: BenFranklinDuplessis.jpg/Wikimedia Commons; p. 27 Everett-Art/Shutterstock.com; p. 29 National Portrait Gallery, Washington/YwG4HdRB_hMBIA at Google Cultural Institute/File: John Trumbull - Alexander Hamilton – Download Google Art Project.jpg/Wikimedia Commons; p. 31 http://www.hallofgovernors.ny.gov/GeorgeClinton/File: George Clinton, governor of New York Download (portrait by Ezra Ames).png/Wikimedia Commons; pp. 34, 41 North Wind Picture Archives; p. 37 Alistair Scott/Shutterstock.com; p. 40 Breamore House, Hampshire, UK/ Bridgeman Images; p. 44 United States Treasury Bureau of Engraving and Printing (http://www.moneyfactory.com/newmoney/main.cfm/currency/new10)/File: US10dollarbill-Series 2004A.jpg/Wikimedia Commons; p. 49 White House Photographer/White House Press Office (https://twitter.com/WhiteHouse/status/614611810415681536)/File: White House rainbow colors to celebrate June 2015 Download SCOTUS same-sex marriage ruling.jpeg/Wikimedia Commons; p. 54 Iain Masterton/Canopy/Getty Images.

Printed in the United States of America

Contents

Chapter One

Setting the Stage for the Federalist Papers

Often history classes give the impression that with the winning of the Revolutionary War and the defeat of the British in 1783, the United States easily grew and flourished into the nation it is today, with the Founding Fathers working side by side to make it happen. However, in reality, the nation's early years were fraught with disagreements—particularly about how the government should be run.

Starting Out

By 1787, the United States was operating under the Articles of Confederation, the nation's first constitution. This document allowed states independent sovereignty under a weak central government. However, because of the Articles, the new

Opposite: (*From left to right*) John Adams, Robert Morris, Alexander Hamilton, and Thomas Jefferson plan the future for what would become the United States.

nation was floundering. Some states were hit harder by the Revolutionary War than others and needed funds to rebuild, but under the Articles of Confederation, the central government could not collect taxes and funnel them into poorer states. Furthermore, they couldn't provide a centralized military force to offer protection against further skirmishes. It became clear to many that something needed to be done. The fledgling United States needed a strong centralized government. More importantly, it needed a constitution.

Garnering Support

To try to build support for a nationally ratified US Constitution, Founding Fathers Alexander Hamilton, John Jay, and James Madison wrote eighty-five letters. To conceal their identities, they published the letters under the pseudonym Publius. The letters they wrote became known as the Federalist Papers. Hamilton, Jay, and Madison sent the letters to newspapers in the late 1780s in the hope of educating the public on matters important to the creation of a country-wide constitution.

However, the story of how the Federalist Papers came to be and their ongoing impact on the US government and its people doesn't start with the Founding Fathers or even the Articles of Confederation. It starts with thirteen British colonies.

The New World

Hundreds of years before the American Revolution, the country was a "new world" to foreign conquerors. To them, it was a land of opportunity, and almost every nation in Europe wanted a piece. The Vikings, it is believed, were the first Europeans to try to build a colony on North American soil, around 1000 CE.

This statue of Leif Eriksson stands in Greenland, but Eriksson was one of the first European explorers to visit the New World.

According to legend, Norse explorer Leif Eriksson heard rumors of a land to the west. He purchased a ship from Bjarni Herjofsson, retraced his route to this alleged new world, and found himself in what is now Canada. There, Eriksson and his crew established a colony called Vinland and set about exploring the local plant and animal life, and acquainting themselves with the New World's native people—probably the Inuit, Innu, and Mi'kmaq tribes.

The colony of Vinland was eventually abandoned, but it planted a seed of possibility for other European nations. From the late 1400s to the mid-1700s, the nations of Portugal, England, Spain, France, the Netherlands, Sweden, and Denmark would all attempt to carve out a piece of that mysterious, fertile land to the west, establishing colonies and setting up trade routes.

Thirteen Colonies

In the 1600s, Great Britain formed two trading companies: the London Company (later the Virginia Company) and the Plymouth Company. In 1606, King James I decreed the Virginia Company would colonize land between the 34th and 41st northern parallel, while the Plymouth Company colonized the region along the eastern seaboard north of that territory. (The Plymouth Company would eventually be absorbed by the Virginia Company.)

In 1607, the Virginia Company founded one of the first successful colonies in the Americas. The settlement was called Jamestown—named after King James I—in what would eventually be the state of Virginia. What makes Jamestown unique when compared to some of the colonies that came before it is that there the settlers established a representative government. The Virginia House of Burgesses consisted of a governor (appointed by the king), a council, and twenty-two representatives from surrounding towns and plantations. As more colonies were settled in coming years and decades, charters were created, establishing this type of governing body. Charters also determined colony boundaries, which often involved absorbing or pushing out colonies established by other countries. By 1735, thirteen individual English colonies had been founded, the last being Georgia in 1732.

Life was more challenging in the northern colonies that would eventually become the states of New Hampshire, Massachusetts, Rhode Island, and Connecticut. All colonies relied on farming to feed families and for trade. However, in the north, winters were colder and crops grew in less abundance

This map shows the original thirteen British colonies.

because the soil was rocky and the growing season was shorter. Northern farmers raised crops of beans, squash, pumpkins, and corn, and, being close to the ocean, they also traded fish for goods. In the middle colonies—later Pennsylvania, New York, New Jersey, and Delaware—the land was more fertile, and colonists grew grains like wheat, barley, and corn. In the southern colonies—Maryland, Virginia, North Carolina, South Carolina, and Georgia—tobacco was king. Tobacco was a valuable currency, and it grew in abundance in the south. By the late 1600s, England was importing around 20,000,000 tons (18,143,694 metric tons) of tobacco every year. Tobacco allowed the southern colonies to thrive in a way that the northern colonies couldn't.

Slavery was a big factor in the economy of the southern colonies. Much of the labor that went into growing tobacco relied on African slaves who had been captured and brought to the

Slavery was a shameful cornerstone of early American and colonial life. In this painting, African slaves are brought to the colonies by Dutch slave traders in 1619.

And Furthermore

African slavery was not the first to exist in the Americas. On Christopher Columbus's first voyage to the New World in 1492, he encountered a native people, the Taino, in what is now Cuba. According to Columbus's journal entries at the time, he believed they would make good servants. He sent thousands of the people to Spain to be sold as slaves. Many did not survive the journey. Others were sent to work on plantations or died of illnesses brought by the colonists.

colonies against their will. The first twenty African slaves arrived in Jamestown in 1619, brought there by Dutch colonists. (Some records have this as being an English ship, despite John Rolfe's account of the event, which may have been purposefully misleading.) According to the Gilder Lehrman Institute, by the 1690s, eighty-five thousand African slaves were being brought to the Americas each year. This number increased by tens of thousands over the next century. Slavery existed in the northern and middle colonies as well, but the economy of these colonies wasn't dependent upon slave labor.

Setting the Stage of War

Tension had been building since the mid-1700s between the American colonies and the British Crown. Colonists were British citizens, but they did not have the same rights as the British people. They did not have representation in Parliament, for instance, and taxes were increasing without the colonists having any say in the proceedings. Britain was in debt because of the European-wide Seven Years' War (1756–1763) and used

Here, a colonist reads a proclamation about the tax on tea. Placing a high tax on goods like tea in the colonies was one way the British government hoped to recover financial losses as a result of the Seven Years' War.

the American colonies as a valuable source of income. One way to increase British coffers was to impose high taxes on some of the American colonies' imports. The Sugar Act of 1764 imposed a tax on sugar. The Stamp Act, passed in 1765, required that all printed materials—newspapers, playing cards, etc.—and any legal documents had to bear a stamp, for which the colonists were required to pay a tax. The Townshend Acts of 1767 placed taxes on glass, lead, paints, paper, and tea.

But the Tea Act of 1773 was the breaking point for many colonists. The East India Company, responsible for trade with Southeast Asia and India and an important part of the British economy at the time, was failing financially. The British government's solution was to grant the company the ability to monopolize tea sales within the colonies and then raise taxes on the tea. A group of colonists, known as the Sons of Liberty, rebelled by boarding three East India Company ships and dumping 342 chests of tea into the Boston Harbor—the destroyed cargo would be worth around $1.7 million today. The monarchy responded by imposing a stricter set of rules in Massachusetts, which colonists called the Intolerable Acts. These acts would close the harbor until the British had been repaid for the destroyed tea, impose a military government, make it more difficult for citizens to get a fair trial, and allow British troops to live in and take control of colonists' personal dwellings.

War Breaks Out

In the aftermath of the Boston Tea Party, as the Sons of Liberty's antics became known, a group of colonists met in September 1774 to discuss what should be done. The colonists in attendance included George Washington, John Adams, Samuel Adams,

Patrick Henry, and John Jay. This meeting would become the gathering of the First Continental Congress. During this meeting, fifty-six delegates from all of the colonies, except Georgia, would meet to draft a rough "declaration of rights and grievances" against Britain. The Continental Congress would meet again (referred to by then as the Second Continental Congress) in late May 1775, joined by Benjamin Franklin and Thomas Jefferson. This time the group would vote to form a continental army, putting Washington in place as the commander. But by then, violence had broken out between the colonies and Great Britain.

Tension was at its height between Britain and the colonies in April 1775, and British troops had orders to suppress any kind of rebellious behavior encountered. On April 18, British general Thomas Gage—the newly appointed royal governor of Massachusetts—ordered British troops to seize a cache of weapons in Concord, a small town about 20 miles (32 kilometers)

The Battle of Lexington marked the first outbreak of violence in the conflict between the British government and the American colonies.

And Furthermore

Before Paul Revere could reach Concord, he was captured by British troops. Documents have revealed that the revolutionaries actually knew about the British plans weeks in advance because of some well-placed spies in the British ranks. Paul Revere has received credit for delivering the information because of Henry Wadsworth Longfellow's poem "Paul Revere's Ride," which is mostly fiction. However, there were people more than just him passing the information along.

from Boston. However, the weapons and other supplies were long gone because, according to popular legend, Paul Revere carried news of the attack to colonial troops the night before. On their way to Concord, seven hundred British troops were met by around seventy militiamen in the town of Lexington. It was there that the first shot of the American Revolution was fired on the morning of April 19, 1775.

A Call for the Declaration of Independence

Not everyone who lived in the American colonies supported the idea of American independence. Those who were loyal to the British crown—some 15 to 20 percent of the population—were called "Tories" or "Loyalists." Britain was, at the time, the most powerful empire in the world. Did the American revolutionaries even stand a chance for victory? Many Loyalists still felt a sense of patriotism toward Britain. Others owned and operated businesses that were aided by British citizenship, like merchants who relied on trade with Britain. So the idea of declaring independence from Great Britain wasn't a universally loved idea in the colonies. It wasn't even the original plan.

When war broke out, it was considered a struggle for rights under the British Crown, but as it raged on, reconciliation seemed unlikely under the circumstances. To many, the idea of independence seemed the logical course.

In January 1776, a writer named Thomas Paine published a pamphlet called *Common Sense*, establishing an argument for American independence. The pamphlet sold over five hundred thousand copies and greatly influenced thoughts of an independent nation in those who read it.

In June of that year, Richard Henry Lee from Virginia formally proposed the idea of declaring independence to Congress, but not all of the colonies agreed. In fact, New York, New Jersey, Delaware, Maryland, and South Carolina opposed it. In the initial vote held at the time, thirty delegates voted for independence, thirty-five voted against it, and sixty-five abstained from voting. The Americans who longed for independence needed a solid plan to help convince others that this was the right move.

The Founding Fathers declared American independence on July 4, 1776, with the signing of the Declaration of Independence.

Thomas Jefferson, John Adams, Benjamin Franklin, Robert Livingston, and Roger Sherman—called the Committee of Five—met several times during the next several weeks to draft an official declaration of independence from Great Britain (Jefferson wrote the bulk of the document, edited by the others). A month later, on July 4, the Continental Congress officially adopted the Declaration of Independence. This time, only John Dickinson, a representative from Delaware who had fought against the Townshend and Stamp Acts the previous decade, opposed it. He believed that the colonies were not ready for war and would be defeated. He abstained from voting to allow Congress to have a unanimous vote for independence. On September 9, 1776, what had become known as the United Colonies was officially renamed the United States of America—not an officially established independent country yet, but this did put the plan in action.

A New Nation

Uniting thirteen states under one central government was never going to be an easy task. There was a divide borne of economic and ideological differences that grew from the very founding of the colonies. Among the issues was the practice of slavery. It was becoming more controversial in some states, and the economy that had been built around it in the Southern states was at risk of collapse if it were to be abolished.

The Articles of Confederation were first adopted by the Continental Congress in 1777 as a way to give the states a centralized government. This was the very first constitution, ratified in 1781. The document was made up of thirteen separate "articles," or rules, which determined the power of the central government and the rights retained by the individual states. From the third article: "The said States hereby severally enter into a firm league of friendship with each other, for their common defense, the security of their liberties, and their mutual and general welfare, binding themselves to assist each other, against all force offered to, or attacks made upon them, or any of them, on account of religion, sovereignty, trade, or any other pretense whatever." This type of alliance among the states is known as a confederacy, where states govern themselves under a loose central government.

The other articles laid out how voting would take place, allowing for equal representation of each state, where funds would come from for handling war with foreign governments or to pay debts. A system of taxation was put into place, but was a sticking point for the Southern states because the original draft required that taxes be paid based on the number of inhabitants in each state. This meant that the Southern states would have

On October 19, 1781, British general Charles Cornwallis (*center on horseback*) surrendered to General George Washington (*right*). The war was over.

to pay taxes based on the number of white residents, as well as slaves. Eventually, it was decided that all states would pay taxes based on the value of their land and economy.

The American Revolution had raged for six years by this time. Fighting finally ended with the surrender of British general Charles Cornwallis to George Washington after the Battle of Yorktown in 1781. Although they were well trained and numerous, the British forces were no match for the scrappy American minutemen, their guerilla warfare tactics, and their knowledge of local geography.

Now, not only did the United States have a government in place, but they would be officially free from British control with the signing of the Treaty of Paris in 1783.

The Imperfect Articles

The Articles of Confederation would be the law of the land for several years after they were ratified. But they were imperfect as a governing document for the United States. Over time, many began to see some of the downsides of the articles. For instance, there wasn't a judicial system in place or a president. There was no central authority except Congress, and they didn't have the power to actually enforce certain laws, especially those surrounding taxation of states to cover national debts and to round up troops for a united army. Many soldiers in the Continental Army received no compensation at all for their military service, but debt collectors were knocking at their doors anyway, demanding payment. Pleas for debt relief went unanswered. Finally, Daniel Shays, a soldier who had fought in the revolution, led one of several uprisings of farmers and other former soldiers in eastern Massachusetts. Shays and his

As part of Shays's Rebellion, lasting from 1786 to 1787, rebels seized control of a Massachusetts courthouse, as shown in this engraving.

comrades were met by 1,200 militiamen, and four of Shays's allies were killed. The series of rebellions would be written in history books as Shays's Rebellion.

Divided and self-governing, the states were weak and acting in their own self-interests. Violence was beginning to take hold. Something needed to happen, and soon, or the nation would fail and everything that the united Americans had fought for would be lost.

The Final Push: The Annapolis Convention

In early 1786, Alexander Hamilton and James Madison were both concerned about issues involving interstate commerce. The states of Virginia and Maryland were in a deadlock over the use of the rivers that ran through both states. Main issues were which state should have control over the waterways when it came to trade and which state should profit from the use of a certain river. Under the Articles of Confederation, states could make their own rules about this type of concern. There was nothing the federal government could do to help settle the argument or instill regulations. To address these concerns, Madison called for a convention: the Annapolis Convention, which would take place in September 1786. Unfortunately, not all of the delegates who were slated to attend felt that the issue was as important as Hamilton and Madison did. Not many actually showed up, and some arrived late.

While not a large convention, the Annapolis Convention was very important for one big reason: it moved George Washington to action. Washington was happily retired at his estate, Mount Vernon, and did not attend the Annapolis Convention. However, the hero of the American Revolution had a long reach politically. The Annapolis Convention brought the issue of interstate commerce to the forefront, and Washington could see that centralized government was the only way to correct this issue. In November, he wrote to Madison, "The consequences of a lax, or inefficient government, are too obvious to be dwelt on. Thirteen Sovereignties pulling against each other and all tugging the federal head, will soon bring ruin on the whole."

While the Annapolis Convention was small in size, it set the stage for the next step: a constitution and the efforts of Alexander Hamilton, James Madison, and John Jay to get it ratified.

Chapter Two

The Federalist Papers Take Their Place in History

The original task of the Constitutional Convention, which began on May 25, 1787, was to revise the existing Articles of Confederation to help strengthen the central government, but as the convention got under way, it became clear that this plan might not go far enough.

The Virginia Plan and Other Proposals

First of all, James Madison arrived with a plan of his own. Called the Virginia Plan, it was essentially a blueprint for a completely new type of government, one that would do away with the Articles of Confederation. Under Madison's plan, states with

Opposite: Despite his desire to enjoy a much-needed retirement, George Washington attended and spoke before the Constitutional Convention. There he would be named the first US president.

larger populations, like Virginia (Madison's home state), would have more power than states with smaller populations.

Madison was not the only delegate with ideas. William Paterson, a delegate from the state of New Jersey, brought in a plan of his own as well. The New Jersey Plan would give each state a single vote in Congress, and this would equalize the power of states large and small.

It was Alexander Hamilton who presented a third plan for a new form of government, one that borrowed from the British constitution and would establish two houses within the legislative branch.

Following much debate, these three plans were combined into one. There would be two legislative houses, one that represented each state equally and one where the number of representatives was determined by population. There would be an executive branch, overseen by an elected president, and a judicial branch, which would help to interpret and enforce the law. In order to regulate power across the three branches, there would be a system of checks and balances put in place.

After several months of debate, by September the framers of the US Constitution had composed a final draft, and it was signed by thirty-nine of fifty-five delegates. But the work of essentially overthrowing and replacing the current government was just beginning. In order for the US Constitution to be the law of the land, it had to be ratified by nine out of thirteen states. By December, only five states—Delaware, Pennsylvania, New Jersey, Georgia, and Connecticut—had ratified the Constitution. A great deal of work still lay ahead for those who supported the document and wanted to see it ratified—and those who didn't.

Opposing Sides

The Constitution was a controversial document. Even those who created it and supported its ratification knew it wasn't going to fix everything. Benjamin Franklin said at the time, "I agree to this Constitution with all its faults, if they are such, because I think a central government is necessary for us ... I doubt too whether any other Convention we can obtain may be able to make a better Constitution." Essentially, in the opinion of many of the Constitution's supporters, even an imperfect constitution was better than the Articles of Confederation.

This portrait of Benjamin Franklin shows him at age seventy-nine, a few years before the Constitutional Convention met.

In the debates surrounding the Constitution, there were two distinct sides. On one side were the Federalists, who believed in a strong central government and wanted the Constitution to be ratified. The Anti-Federalists—a name they did not give themselves, but one that was given to them for simply opposing the Federalists—strongly supported states' rights, and while many of them were supportive of a constitution, they wanted to ensure that individual rights would be protected under the new rule of law. They worried that the new form of government would once again place Americans under the tyrannical rule that they had experienced under the British.

There was also a firm divide between those who supported slavery and those who opposed it. The economy of the United States had been built around and relied upon slavery, particularly

And Furthermore

James Madison was an abolitionist, meaning that he was against slavery. He expressed his discomfort with the practice in both essay forty-two and essay fifty-four of the Federalist Papers. This stand was hypocritical, however, as Madison himself owned slaves. In essay fifty-four, he argued that the Three-Fifths Compromise was one of the strengths of the Constitution, since it worked to protect individual "property." However, he viewed the practice as inhumane and supported the plan to revisit abolition in 1808, as outlined in the Constitution. Despite this, upon his death in 1836, Madison did not free his slaves in his will.

in the Southern states. The Declaration of Independence stated that "all men are created equal," and yet the practice of slavery existed and continued to thrive in the United States. However, antislavery movements were beginning to gain a foothold.

During the Constitutional Convention, as the formation of the legislative branch was being discussed, many questioned how the slave population in the South would be counted in determining state representation. If the slaves were counted, the Southern states would have more officials in the House of Representatives, allowing them to dominate votes in their favor. In order to avoid this imbalance, the Three-Fifths Compromise was proposed, counting every slave as only three-fifths of a person. The question of the rights of slaves also arose. Since states could pass abolition laws individually, what would happen to slaves who escaped to free states? In drafting the Constitution, the Founding Fathers included an article that required escaped slaves to be returned to their owners. There was also a provision that the import of slaves might be banned by Congress after 1808. For antislavery advocates like Alexander Hamilton, John Jay, and Benjamin Franklin, these compromises went against their principles but were necessary to help gain favor for the Constitution.

The Federalists

Of all of the Founding Fathers who considered themselves to be Federalists, three stand out as the most influential of the group: Alexander Hamilton, James Madison, and John Jay. It was these three who wrote and published the Federalist Papers, under the pseudonym Publius. Of course, the information about the true authors' identities was kept secret, at least until Hamilton's death in 1804 (although it's said that this was not a well-kept secret).

Federalist Papers coauthor James Madison in 1821

The Federalist Papers were a work of propaganda, so while being outspoken in polite debate was acceptable, writing an appeal to the public for support might be considered unethical and in violation of the confidentiality of the Constitutional Convention.

After graduating from the College of New Jersey (now known as Princeton), James Madison, like many of his peers, became interested in the relationship between the American colonies and Britain, particularly issues surrounding taxation. He spent time studying other governments from around the world, and when the new constitution came up for debate, he drew one basic conclusion: America needed a strong central government. Madison is often called the "Father of the Constitution" because he wrote the Constitution's first ten amendments, called the Bill of Rights. Likewise, it was Madison who suggested the system of checks and balances between branches of government.

John Jay was an outspoken advocate of the Constitution. He would go on to be named the first justice of the Supreme Court.

Before the American Revolution, John Jay was actually opposed to declaring independence from Britain, instead working for reconciliation until that option became impossible. Jay's role was often that of a peacemaker, acting as the American minister to Spain and later joining the American peace commission. John Jay contributed five essays to the collected Federalist Papers. His efforts were cut short by illness.

Alexander Hamilton was born in the British-controlled West Indies (now the Caribbean) on the small island of Nevis in 1755. His father, James Hamilton, was a Scottish tradesman, and his mother, Rachel, was the wife of a merchant. Being born out of wedlock at this time was a huge breach of decorum, and children born in these circumstances were often relegated to a life of second-class citizenship. In 1765, James Hamilton abandoned his family, and just three years later, Rachel died, leaving Alexander without parents. However, young Hamilton was smart and driven. He would become a clerk at a trading firm, Beekman and Cruger, by age fourteen, and a manager by the age of seventeen. Seeing his talent, the residents of St. Croix took up a collection to send Hamilton to the mainland to further his education. In America, Hamilton studied the law at King's College in New York. But the seeds of revolution were planted all around him, and it wasn't long until the smart and driven man became involved in politics.

Alexander Hamilton was the chief planner behind the Federalist Papers.

During the revolution, George Washington took notice of Hamilton's skills and hired him as an assistant and advisor. His outspoken nature earned him a spot among the other delegates at the Constitutional Convention. Alexander Hamilton contributed fifty-one of the collected Federalist Papers.

The Anti-Federalists

The biggest challenge that the Federalists faced was opposition. There were those who opposed the Constitution, the Anti-Federalists. Some of the most well-known Anti-Federalists were Patrick Henry, Samuel Adams, George Mason of Virginia, and Governor George Clinton of New York.

Patrick Henry is often considered the father of the Anti-Federalist movement, as he was one of the first politicians to openly oppose the Constitution. Before the American Revolution, Patrick Henry was strongly opposed to British tyranny. He had openly argued against the Stamp Act, to the point where many considered his words to be treasonous. He wanted to avoid the type of control the British government had had over the colonies. He was a strong leader, and many rallied behind him.

The Anti-Federalists distributed pamphlets, gave speeches, and wrote essays of their own, citing their reasons for opposing the Constitution. Henry was very influential as a voice for the Anti-Federalists, but for Alexander Hamilton, his biggest opponent was George Clinton, the governor of his adopted state.

The Federalists' Plan

The Federalist Papers were not originally intended to be influential across all thirteen states. They were directed at the

New York governor George Clinton was one of the leading Anti-Federalists of the time. As governor, he was very popular and a strong leader.

people of New York. Soon after the Constitutional Convention, a New York-based newspaper called the *Daily Advertiser* published a report on what the new constitution contained, and many New Yorkers were shocked and unhappy. This was a completely different government and a huge departure from just updating the Articles of Confederation. New York was big, populous, and a major center of trade and commerce, so it was important to convince the people of New York that the Constitution needed to be ratified. One of the most outspoken opponents of the Constitution was the Anti-Federalist New York governor George Clinton. Therefore, getting New York to ratify was going to be an enormous challenge. For several weeks, in the summer and fall of 1787, newspapers were filled with Federalist and Anti-Federalist opinion pieces. The governor even authored a series of essays under the name Cato, strongly objecting to the Constitution.

Alexander Hamilton was never the type to take criticism easily, especially criticism of something he believed in as strongly as he believed in the Constitution. He fought fire with fire, responding to Clinton's letters by penning his own, signed "Caesar."

Then in October 1787, he came up with a plan for a writing project that would truly outshine "Cato's" Anti-Federalist writings. He would compose a series of essays that would explain, in detail, the need for a stronger central government. Then it would outline how the Constitution would fit that role. But Hamilton couldn't take on the entire project himself. He needed help.

The first writer Hamilton approached was John Jay, who quickly agreed. Then, he spoke to James Madison, who also agreed. Hamilton's intention was to involve the framers of the Constitution because their insight was very valuable. This is why Hamilton also approached William Duer and Gouverneur Morris, New York statesmen who had been a part of the Constitutional Convention. But both declined. Nonetheless, with Jay and Madison on board, Hamilton's plan was under way.

John Jay was the former minister to Spain, so his essays would focus on foreign relations. James Madison, who had authored the Virginia Plan, would explain the basics of the new government structure. And Hamilton would compose essays on military issues, taxation, and the executive and judicial branches of government.

The First Letter

Alexander Hamilton took on the task of writing the first of the Federalist Papers, which was published in the *New York Independent Journal* on October 27, 1787. The letter opened with, "After an unequivocal experience of the inefficiency of the subsisting federal government, you are called upon to deliberate on a new Constitution for the United States of America." Hamilton's words were a call for debate, and they sought to inform:

> *It has until lately been a received and uncontradicted opinion that the prosperity of the people of America depended on their continuing firmly united, and the wishes, prayers, and efforts of our best and wisest citizens have been constantly directed to that object. But politicians now appear, who insist that this opinion is erroneous, and that instead of looking for safety and happiness in union, we ought to seek it in a division of the States into distinct confederacies or sovereignties.*

They explained where the divisions were and why they existed.

The first of the Federalist Papers set a tone for what was to come from the rest of the letters signed Publius:

> *For nothing can be more evident, to those who are able to take an enlarged view of the subject, than the*

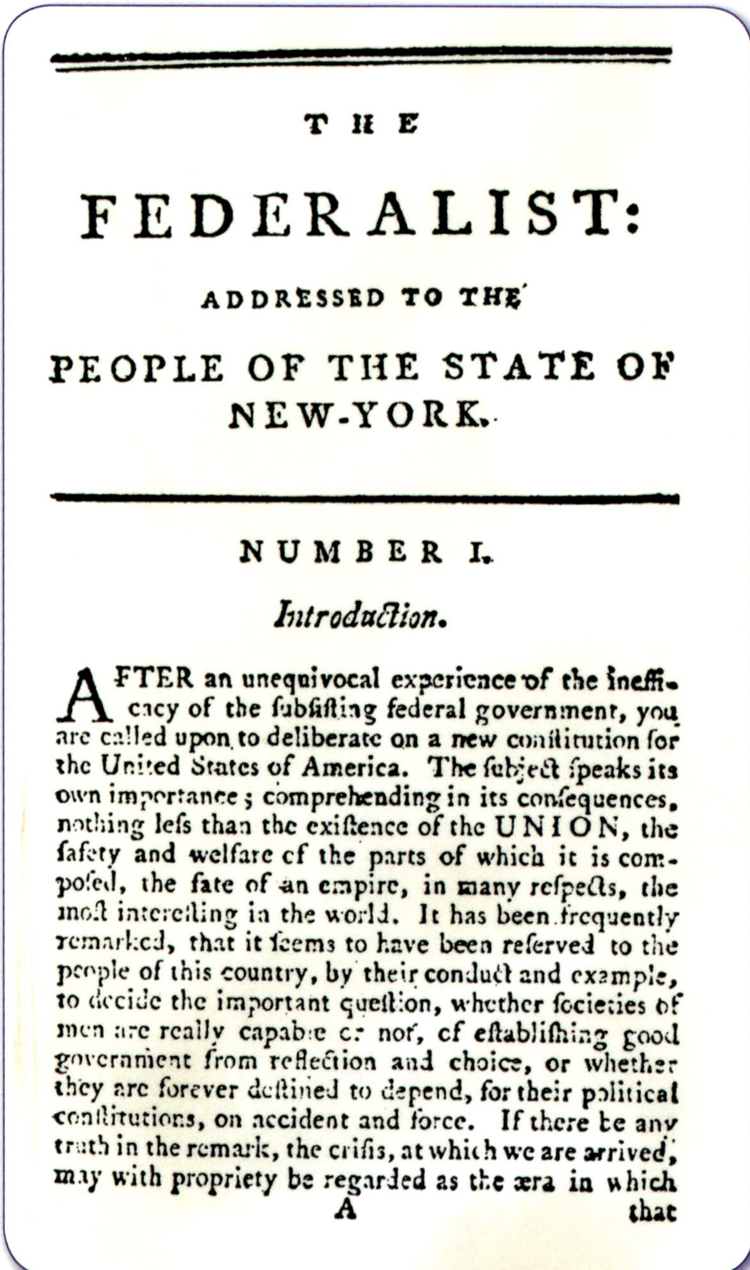

THE

FEDERALIST:

ADDRESSED TO THE

PEOPLE OF THE STATE OF NEW-YORK.

NUMBER I.

Introduction.

AFTER an unequivocal experience of the inefficacy of the subsisting federal government, you are called upon to deliberate on a new constitution for the United States of America. The subject speaks its own importance; comprehending in its consequences, nothing less than the existence of the UNION, the safety and welfare of the parts of which it is composed, the fate of an empire, in many respects, the most interesting in the world. It has been frequently remarked, that it seems to have been reserved to the people of this country, by their conduct and example, to decide the important question, whether societies of men are really capable or not, of establishing good government from reflection and choice, or whether they are forever destined to depend, for their political constitutions, on accident and force. If there be any truth in the remark, the crisis, at which we are arrived, may with propriety be regarded as the æra in which

A that

The Federalist Papers are often still referenced today as some of the best, most comprehensive documents in favor of the Constitution.

alternative of an adoption of the new Constitution or a dismemberment of the Union. It will therefore be of use to begin by examining the advantages of that Union, the certain evils, and the probable dangers, to which every State will be exposed from its dissolution. This shall accordingly constitute the subject of my next address.

In 1787, news did not travel the way it does today, so there is not a way to gauge the initial public reaction to the first letter before the second, penned by John Jay, followed a few days later. However, a letter from George Washington to Alexander Hamilton dated November 10, 1787, acknowledges that Washington knew the identity of Publius: "I thank you for the Pamphlet and for the Gazette contained in your letter of the 30th Ult. For the remaining numbers of Publius, I shall acknowledge myself obliged, as I am persuaded the subject will be well handled by the Author." He goes on to say, however, that he stands with the majority, meaning that he is reluctant to take sides in the debate until there is a strong majority on one side or the other. But whether Washington was being coy or was actually still unconvinced to take a side at the time he penned that letter, he eventually did come forward in support of the Constitution. He was such a respected figure that his support did a lot to persuade others.

A Flurry of Letters

For the next seven months, the essays continued to appear regularly on the pages of the *New York Independent Journal*. Essays two through five were written by John Jay, and served as a bit of a lesson on the importance of a central government over a loose confederation of states. One of the biggest reasons Jay cited was safety of the American people from foreign invaders. In the third of the Federalist Papers, he says, "Among the many objects to which a wise and free people find it necessary to direct their attention, that of providing for their SAFETY seems to be the first. The SAFETY of the people doubtless has relation to a great variety of circumstances and considerations, and consequently affords great latitude to those who wish to define it precisely and comprehensively." A country united under a larger central government would have better resources for creating a military, rather than relying on militia units in each state.

And Furthermore

In a letter dated August 28, 1788, in the months after the Constitution was ratified, George Washington wrote to Hamilton to say, "I will say, that I have seen no other so well calculated (in my judgment) to produce conviction on an unbiased Mind, as the Production of your triumvirate." The "triumvirate" he's referring to is the trio of Hamilton, Jay, and Madison. He was acknowledging the influence the Federalist Papers had on those who had not been swayed in favor of the Constitution before reading them.

John Jay also used Great Britain as an example of why a divided nation is weaker, writing in the fifth of the Federalist Papers, "The history of Great Britain is the one with which we are in general the best acquainted, and it gives us many useful lessons ... Although it seems obvious to common sense that the people of such an

Great Britain, whose flag is shown here, had for centuries faced uprisings and civil war among the British people. John Jay wanted the United States to avoid that type of existence.

island should be but one nation, yet we find that they were for ages divided into three"—here he was referring to England, Wales, and Scotland (the countries that form Great Britain)—"and that those three were almost constantly embroiled in quarrels and wars with one another. Notwithstanding their true interest with respect to the continental nations was really the same, yet by the arts and policy and practices of those nations, their mutual jealousies were perpetually kept inflamed, and for a long series of years they were far more inconvenient and troublesome than they were useful and assisting to each other." England had long been caught up in fights with Scotland, Ireland, and Wales for control of those lands, in addition to the war with the American colonies they had just lost.

Madison's Plea Against Factions

James Madison's first contribution to the Federalist Papers was the tenth essay of the collection. This essay is one of the most well-known and highly regarded. Madison established with this work that the nation at that time was divided into factions—meaning groups that were united under a single interest or by property ownership or wealth. Members of these factions were acting in their own self-interests to further their own goals, without any regard for the rest of the nation. Madison suggested that cutting off the freedom to act in one's self-interests would help unite the American people under the same interests: "In the extent and proper structure of the Union, therefore, we behold a republican remedy for the diseases most incident to republican government. And according to the degree of pleasure and pride we feel in being republicans, ought to be our zeal in cherishing the spirit and supporting the character of Federalists." (By "republicans," Madison is referring not to the political party of today, but simply to those who support a republic government—one made up of elected officials and not a monarch.)

Hamilton Explains It All

In the fifteenth essay of the Federalist Papers (and up through essay twenty-two, although Madison is co-credited for essays eighteen to twenty), Hamilton changed the message a bit. In the previous essays, Hamilton, Jay, and Madison discussed the importance of a union in regards to "political safety and happiness." In the fifteenth essay, however, Hamilton discussed the weaknesses of the Articles of Confederation, arguing that individual states ruling themselves leads to a nation of individual

An Underwhelming Success

In 1788, Archibald McLean was the New York-based printer Alexander Hamilton hired to publish the complete works of the Federalist Papers in book form. However, he had agreed to publish around twenty to twenty-five essays, not eighty-five. The project had ballooned in size over the course of several months, meaning that the agreed-upon rate for five hundred copies was no longer sufficient to cover the cost of printing. The project ended up costing McLean £220 (about $33,000 today). The printed version was published in two volumes. However, it did not sell as well as expected, so McLean was stuck with about two hundred unsold copies. These unsold copies would eventually, comically, become the second edition published in 1799 by John Tieboult.

Despite the lack of initial sales, the Federalist Papers did eventually have success, but not most noticeably until the nineteenth century when people began to revisit one of the greatest works of American history. In the twenty-first century, it remains in print.

sovereignties: "The measures of the Union have not been executed; the delinquencies of the States have, step by step, matured themselves to an extreme, which has, at length, arrested all the wheels of the national government, and brought them to an awful stand." There is also a tone of fear that this kind of division could lead to civil war, weakening the union even more.

Portraits often portray Alexander Hamilton near a quill and parchment. This portrait shows a close-up of his hand.

Essay twenty-three is the first to offer an alternative to the Articles of Confederation: the Constitution. This essay and those that followed it also sum up the responsibilities of a government and how the Constitution would see these tasks done. Hamilton discusses the distribution of power among the three branches of government and how a united military force would help provide protection for the entire nation. In the essays following this summary, Publius goes into greater detail, breaking down the powers of the legislative branch, in essays fifty-two to sixty-five. Essays sixty-seven through seventy-seven discuss the powers of the executive branch, and the judicial department is broken down in detail from seventy-eight to eighty-three. Essentially, everything anyone would ever need to know about the new Constitution was carefully outlined in essays twenty-three through eighty-three.

The Constitution Becomes Law

No one can really say if Publius's writings were the deciding factor in the last needed vote to ratify the Constitution, but several copies of the bound works were sent to the Virginia Ratifying Convention, which took place on June 26, 1788, where Patrick Henry and James Madison were both in attendance. In

In New York, crowds celebrated the ratification of the Constitution with a parade in Alexander Hamilton's honor.

reality, the Federalist Papers were only a fraction of the work being done on both sides to sway the vote in their favor. Some argue that the promised addition of the Bill of Rights—drafted by James Madison and added officially on December 15, 1791—was what swayed the votes of Massachusetts, Maryland, South Carolina, and New Hampshire. Regardless, on June 21, 1788, nine states had officially ratified the document, making the US Constitution the law of the land starting in March 1789. The other states slowly followed. The only exception was the state of Rhode Island, but the government threatened to cut ties with the state, which would damage its economy, so the state at last voted to ratify on May 29, 1790, bringing all thirteen states officially into the union under the Constitution.

Congress met officially for the first time on March 4, 1789, and there were enormous tasks ahead of them, as creating laws that actually enforced the Constitution were key to the success of the new government. Congress also named George Washington the first president of the United States, establishing the executive branch for the first time. Being in Congress back then was not an enviable experience, however. Members were constantly traveling between Philadelphia, New York City, and their home states, meaning a lot of time away from families. One-third of the Senate resigned during the 1790s.

The Final Paper

The final essay of the Federalist Papers was published in August 1788—a few months after New Hampshire ratified the Constitution, completing the needed nine votes, although a few states, including the Federalist Papers' intended target, New York, had still not reached an agreement.

Written by Alexander Hamilton, the final letter repeated the importance of a central government, stating, "A nation, without a national government, is, in my view, an awful spectacle. The establishment of a Constitution, in time of profound peace, by the voluntary consent of a whole people, is a prodigy, to the completion of which I look forward with trembling anxiety." With these words, Hamilton's job was done. Even though the Constitution had been ratified, he made it clear there was still work to do to ensure that the public understood it was the right move.

THE UNITED STATES OF AMERICA TEN DOLLARS THE UNITED STATES OF AMERICA
HAMILTON

Chapter Three

The Federalist Papers in Modern Society

On July 11, 1804, Alexander Hamilton was killed in a duel with political rival Aaron Burr. The legacy that he built during his life is often overshadowed by the tragedy and suddenness of his death. But Alexander Hamilton achieved so much during his short life that we are still seeing and experiencing the effects of it today. As the first secretary of the treasury, he founded the entire US financial system, including the US mint, taxation, and debt management, and he established the dollar as currency. He started the Revenue Cutter Service, a tax collection bureau that would eventually become the US Coast Guard. Hamilton also started a daily broadsheet—a large-sized newspaper format—that would eventually become the *New York Post*. He even appears today on the ten-dollar bill. But most important

Opposite: The first secretary of the treasury, Alexander Hamilton, is commemorated on the ten-dollar bill.

of everything he left behind were his contributions to the Federalist Papers.

These eighty-five essays continue to be the most comprehensive, detailed explanation of the Constitution as it existed at the time, and people still reference them today. In January 1999, then Democratic Senator from Arkansas Dale Bumpers recommended that members of President Bill Clinton's impeachment hearing read essay sixty-five of the Federalist Papers—regarding the Senate's role in impeachment proceedings—before voting on a decision. The next day, Amazon.com reported increased sales of the historical documents—and Bill Clinton was not removed from office.

Essay sixty-eight is often in the news during and after an election year because it outlines and defends the use of an electoral college in electing a president. In 1824, 1876, 1886, 2000, and 2016, the winner of the electoral college vote lost the popular vote. So many are still debating Hamilton's opinion on the benefits of the electoral college over two hundred years after he wrote about it.

The Two-Party System

The writing of the Federalist Papers and the ratification of the Constitution marked one of the last times that James Madison and Alexander Hamilton agreed politically. As the first US secretary of the treasury, Hamilton was tasked with creating a whole financial system for the United States. The federal government and states were already millions of dollars in debt because of the American Revolution. Hamilton's plan was to get the states out of debt by having the federal government absorb that debt, which many felt was unfair. Some states, like Virginia,

This portrait of Thomas Jefferson was completed in 1788. As secretary of state, Jefferson was opposed to Hamilton's financial plan as he felt it gave the federal government too much power.

carried less debt than others. Virginians Thomas Jefferson and James Madison immediately opposed the plan, as they felt it showed overreach of the federal government.

This disagreement ultimately led to the formation of two distinctive political parties, the Federalists and the Democratic-Republicans. This type of political system is known as a "two-party system," in which each party works toward electing a majority in Congress in order to create laws that align with the principles of that party. The most prominent political parties today are the Republican and Democratic Parties.

The legacy of the Federalist Papers continues to live on in both parties and the lives of US citizens. As a political document, the Federalist Papers are ingrained in the history of the United States and in the earliest acts of political compromise and decision-making. Today, Americans continue to disagree on some of the same topics they disagreed on over two hundred years ago—states' rights, enforcing policy, the right to bear arms, and more. Let's take a look at some recent issues that divided Americans the way the Constitution once did.

Twenty-First-Century American Politics

Although the names of the political parties have changed and their key issues have evolved, the divide is still essentially the same today as it was at the founding of the nation. The roles of the central government and individual state governments continue to shift, and deciding if issues should be handled at the state or federal level continues to come into question regularly. With the institution of slavery in the past, rules and regulations regarding same-sex marriage and government-subsidized health care have taken its place.

In June 2015, the US Supreme Court issued a judicial order that same-sex couples be allowed to marry in all fifty states and US territories, overruling state bans of the practice in Arkansas, Georgia, Michigan, Kansas, Texas, and others. Many

After the Supreme Court legalized marriage equality across the United States in 2015, the White House was lit with the traditional LGBTQ rainbow.

argued that the federal government overstepped its authority in doing this, that individual states should be allowed to vote on the issues and let the people decide their state's policy on same-sex marriage and similar unions.

The issue of same-sex marriage first arrived on the forefront of American politics in 1972 with the Supreme Court case of *Baker v. Nelson*, in which a gay couple—Richard Baker and Michael McConnell—sought the ability to obtain a marriage license in the state of Minnesota. They didn't win, but this opened up an important argument; other couples were soon joining the cause and demanding their right to marry whomever they chose. In 2009, Proposition 8 appeared on the California state ballot, calling for a ban on same-sex marriage in that state. Many who opposed the practice believed it violated their religious freedom.

As with the Constitution many years before, two distinctive sides of the issue developed, and on each side, people worked to draw voters to their cause, using information (and misinformation) to gain support. But unlike Alexander Hamilton, James Madison, and John Jay, modern activists can share their causes via the internet through social media, opinion blogs, and news sources. The powerful phrase "Love is love," rainbow flags, photographs of happy same-sex couples, and similar messages helped to popularize the idea of same-sex marriage. Increased support from the public pushed then president Barack Obama to move in support of it as well.

When the Patient Protection and Affordable Care Act (sometimes referred to as Obamacare) was signed into law in March 2010, attorneys general from a number of states filed suit, calling the bill unconstitutional. The main goal of the Affordable Care Act (ACA) is to extend health-insurance coverage to people who are not covered by employers or by programs for the elderly and the poor. To help Americans afford coverage, the government offers subsidies—a certain amount of money to help defray these costs, provided by taxation. Again, two distinctive sides rose up in support and opposition of the bill. Many Americans feel that it's unfair for them to pay for the medical coverage of others and that it's driving up the operating costs for businesses—which are required to provide insurance coverage if they employ over a certain number of people—and that states should be allowed to opt out of the ACA if they choose. Others argue that health insurance is a right and should be provided to all Americans, even if it adds to the cost for taxpayers, and support the reach of the federal government over state government in enforcing the law.

Again, supporters and opponents of the bill took to social media and online forums to spread their views. Companies and business owners with interest in the insurance industry have also begun to invest in "think tanks" to help find information that will help turn the tide of public opinion, as happened with the same-sex marriage agenda. These agencies create social media accounts and websites and even invest in news organizations to help spread anti- and pro-health-care ideologies, which, if successful, will help that business to be more profitable. This information is a type of propaganda.

American Propaganda

Propaganda is defined as the spread of an idea, image, rumor, or body of information for the purpose of helping promote (or damage) a cause, an organization, or a person or a group of people. It can be truthful or misleading, which is why some propaganda, like the Federalist Papers, are widely hailed, and

"Join, or Die" was one of the first propaganda campaigns in American history. It called for unification in the colonies.

others, like Nazi images spread during the rise of Nazi Germany that portrayed Jews as evil, are condemned.

One of the first important pieces of propaganda in American history was created by Benjamin Franklin: the "Join, or Die" campaign, first published in the *Pennsylvania Gazette* in 1754. The image portrayed the colonies as individual pieces of a snake that would die if it did not put itself back together. This piece was distributed to help unify the thirteen colonies. The image is still seen frequently today. For instance, television personality Craig Ferguson has a tattoo of the political cartoon on his forearm to commemorate becoming a US citizen. The image also makes an appearance in the popular video game *Fallout 4*.

During World War II, the "We Can Do It" image, created by artist J. Howard Miller, sought to recruit women into important wartime jobs abandoned by men off fighting in the war, like working in factories, driving trucks, and fixing cars. The image of "Rosie the Riveter" became an important icon in the war effort. Rosie continues to be an icon for feminism today. The annual Home Front Festival in Richmond, California, even features a Rosie Rally, where attendees arrive dressed as the icon herself.

And Furthermore

The Federalist Papers have a recognizable icon like Rosie the Riveter to carry on their legacy as a recognizable force for change: Alexander Hamilton. The Broadway musical *Hamilton*, based on his life, has popularized Alexander Hamilton as a cultural icon, and even features a song, "Non-Stop," about the time Hamilton spent writing the essays.

Consider the Source

It can be difficult to distinguish between news that has been fact-checked and verified and news that has been fabricated. If you aren't sure if a piece of news is true, check the source using a search engine like Google. Sources like the Associated Press, Reuters, and the *New York Times* tend to be reliable. You can often consult unbiased fact-checking websites like snopes.com for more information about news stories that seem unbelievable. You can also search for the information in the story and see if any legitimate news sites have posted articles on the subject. If nothing comes up, you can usually assume that the news is fake. Finally, check the quality of the writing. Legitimate news sources hire copy editors to proof spelling and grammar. If you notice a lot of typos, you might be reading from an unreliable source.

Propaganda Today

Publius used the medium of newspapers to spread their message, but today, people have access to the internet, which means that ideas—good and bad—can be shared instantly and spread more quickly. Thanks to the internet, people can read bills that are being voted on at both the state and national levels. They can read news and opinions to help them understand the issues better and form opinions of their own. People can even share their viewpoints through blogs and social media.

Some websites could contain false or misleading information. Be sure to take the proper precautions to avoid this type of content.

However, this also means that extremist websites are just a click away, often disguising themselves as partisan—meaning aligned with one particular political party—opinion and news sites. Some of these sites post fabricated news stories to incite outrage. Readers share stories via social media, often without checking the accuracy of the story. Once the story spreads under the guise of fact, it can't be retracted.

If there is anything to be learned from the Federalist Papers, the drafting of the Constitution, and the very founding of the United States, it's that what you say and what you do matter.

Glossary

abolition The movement to end slavery in the United States.

Anti-Federalists A group of politicians opposed to the Constitution, favoring the Articles of Confederation instead.

article A rule, usually outlined officially in a document or contract.

cache A secure location used for hiding important supplies, often in times of war.

checks and balances A system that allows a government to regulate power across the three branches. Bills must pass through all three branches in order to become and remain law.

colony A territory outside of a ruling nation occupied by citizens of that nation, usually to expand trade.

confederacy A group of states that are united under a loose government, but self-governing.

constitution A document that contains the basic laws of a nation, outlining the role of the government and the individual rights of the citizens of that nation.

executive branch The branch of government controlled by an elected president or governor, with the power to sign bills into law or veto them.

Federalist A member of the Federalist Party, believing in a strong central government and a loose interpretation of the US Constitution in creating laws.

judicial branch The branch of government that determines the lawfulness of policies imposed at both the state and national level.

legislative branch The branch of government that creates bills and works to vote them into law.

majority The side of a decision with the larger number of votes.

monarchy Absolute rule by an individual, such as a king or a queen.

partisan Showing loyalty to one particular political party.

propaganda Ideas or facts spread purposefully to engage the public and potentially sway opinion in one's favor.

ratify To approve officially, as with an important political document.

republican Supporting a type of government ruled by an official elected by the citizens of the nation.

revolution A fast upheaval or change, often resulting in the transfer of power within a government.

social media Websites or apps that are used to connect people for the purpose of content sharing.

sovereignty A role of supreme power over a nation, as in a monarchy.

territory A piece of land that is only loosely under the control of a government.

two-party system A system of government controlled by two parties, where each works to gain the majority in order to influence lawmaking to meet policy standards of the party.

Further Information

Books

Chernow, Ron. *Alexander Hamilton*. New York: Penguin Books, 2005.

DK. *The American Revolution: A Visual History*. New York: DK, 2016.

Feldman, Noah. *The Three Lives of James Madison: Genius, Partisan, President*. New York: Random House, 2017.

Hamilton, Alexander, James Madison, and John Jay. *The Federalist Papers: A Collection of Essays Written in Favour of the New Constitution*. Dublin, OH: Coventry House, 2015.

Khan, Khizr. *This Is Our Constitution: Discover America with a Gold Star Father*. New York: Knopf, 2017.

Websites

Biography: Alexander Hamilton

https://www.biography.com/people/alexander-hamilton-9326481

Read this biography on the life of Alexander Hamilton.

The Federalist Papers

https://www.congress.gov/resources/display/content/The+Federalist+Papers

This website allows you to read the Federalist Papers, collected in their entirety.

Gilder Lehrman Institute of American History: Differences Between Federalists and Anti-Federalists

https://www.gilderlehrman.org/content/differences-between-federalists-and-antifederalists

This website breaks down the differences between the Federalists and the Anti-Federalists by using an easy-to-understand chart.

Our Government: The Constitution

https://www.whitehouse.gov/1600/constitution

Here you can find a complete history of the US Constitution and an in-depth explanation of what it says.

Snopes

https://www.snopes.com

This website provides reliable fact-checking services on popular news stories.

Bibliography

"African Americans at Jamestown." National Park Service. https://www.nps.gov/jame/learn/historyculture/african-americans-at-jamestown.htm.

"All Amendments to the United States Constitution." University of Minnesota Human Rights Library. http://hrlibrary.umn.edu/education/all_amendments_usconst.htm.

"Anthony Benezet." PBS.org. http://www.pbs.org/wgbh/aia/part3/3p248.html.

"Articles of Confederation, 1777–1781." Office of the Historian. https://history.state.gov/milestones/1776-1783/articles.

Barnes, Robert. "Supreme Court: Was Gay Marriage Settled in 1972 Case?" *Washington Post*. August 17, 2014. https://www.washingtonpost.com/politics/courts_law/supreme-court-was-gay-marriage-settled-in-1972-case/2014/08/17/1a5e41f8-23c6-11e4-86ca-6f03cbd15c1a_story.html?utm_term=.f90e9f9b4f07.

"Bill of Rights." History.com. http://www.history.com/topics/bill-of-rights.

Chaney, Ted, Ken Cohen, and Lee Pelham Cotton. "The Virginia Company of London." National Park Service. https://www.nps.gov/jame/learn/historyculture/the-virginia-company-of-london.htm.

Chernow, Ron. *Alexander Hamilton*. New York: Penguin, 2005.

"Constitutional Amendment Process." National Archives. https://www.archives.gov/federal-register/constitution.

"Federalist Papers." History.com. http://www.history.com/topics/federalist-papers.

Feldman, Noah. "James Madison's Lessons in Racism." *New York Times*. October 28, 2017. https://www.nytimes.com/2017/10/28/opinion/sunday/james-madison-racism.html.

"Final Speech." PBS.org. http://www.pbs.org/benfranklin/pop_finalspeech.html.

Foner, Eric, and John A. Garraty, eds. "Missouri Compromise." History.com. 1991. http://www.history.com/topics/missouri-compromise.

"George Washington to Alexander Hamilton, August 28, 1788." Library of Congress. https://www.loc.gov/resource/mgw2.015/?sp=262&st=text.

"George Washington to Alexander Hamilton, November 10, 1787." Library of Congress. https://www.loc.gov/resource/mgw2.014/?sp=195&st=text.

Graham, David A. "Can States Ignore the Supreme Court on Gay Marriage?" *Atlantic*, July 1, 2015. https://www.theatlantic.com/politics/archive/2015/07/nullification-again/397373.

Hamilton, Alexander, James Madison, and John Jay. "The Federalist Papers." Yale Law School, The Avalon Project. http://avalon.law.yale.edu/subject_menus/fed.asp.

Hamilton, Allan McLane. *The Intimate Life of Alexander Hamilton*. New York: Scribner's, 1910.

Henry, Patrick. "Patrick Henry, Virginia Ratifying Convention." The Founders' Constitution. http://press-pubs.uchicago.edu/founders/documents/v1ch14s39.html.

"Historical Context: Facts About the Slave Trade and Slavery." The Gilder Lehrman Institute of American History. https://www.gilderlehrman.org/content/historical-context-facts-about-slave-trade-and-slavery.

"James Madison." History.com. http://www.history.com/topics/us-presidents/james-madison.

"John Brown." PBS.org. http://www.pbs.org/wgbh/aia/part4/4p1550.html.

Lucas, Paul R. "Exploration of North America." History.com. http://www.history.com/topics/exploration/exploration-of-north-america.

Mueller, Anne Moore. "John Woolman." BrynMawr.edu. 2008. http://web.tricolib.brynmawr.edu/speccoll/quakersandslavery/commentary/people/woolman.php.

Tilva, Rahul. "Shays' Rebellion." George Washington's Mount Vernon. http://www.mountvernon.org/digital-encyclopedia/article/shays-rebellion.

"Why Is Obamacare So Controversial?" BBC News. July 13, 2017. http://www.bbc.com/news/world-us-canada-24370967.

Index

Page numbers in **boldface** are illustrations.

About the Author

Bethany Bryan is the author of several books, as well as an editor and copy editor. Her previous works include *The Cold War Chronicles: The Bay of Pigs and the Cuban Missile Crisis* and *Leading Women: Melania Trump: Model and First Lady*. She enjoys studying American history and visiting presidential museums, her favorite being Sagamore Hill in Oyster Bay, New York—the home of Theodore Roosevelt. She lives in Kansas City, Missouri.